Human Touch in the Digital Age

Human Touch in the Digital Age

Marlon Shaun

To my best bud, Horace.
What a long, strange trip it has been.

Contents

1 Introduction

It is said that we live in a more democratic society than ever in human history; information has never been more easily available, and the world has never been more open [LR21]. As technological development and digitization advances further, more advanced technology becomes available to the public. Such technology continuously changes the way humans communicate [LR21], especially with the rise of social media and web 2.0[1] where users of the internet have a central role in content creation. Social media has changed how people acquire and share information and these platforms have become an essential source of information to many [YT21]. Oftentimes, content can be created anonymously and published without excessive examination for validity and authenticity [DB18]. This becomes especially problematic when content touches on controversial or emotionally charged topics. The emotional reactions of users contribute to the fast pace at which information spreads, and the sheer volume of information that people are now subjected to makes it very difficult to assess truthfulness [Wet19]

Today, platforms such as Twitter have become a platform for manipulating public opinion and spreading or amplifying political misinformation [SA18]. However, not all communication partners in online interactions are honest interaction partners or even humans. Fully or semi-automated user accounts, so called social bots, participate in online interactions increasingly often [Bir19].

Social bots have become a successor to automated agents, so-called bots. Bots are usually designed to save time and energy of a human author, because they parse and organize information at great speeds, saving human actors from doing the repetitive work [GG18]. Early bots were designed by scientists to perform simple regulatory tasks within closed platforms, but bots were quickly extended beyond platform, performing network maintenance tasks as well as social interactions [RW18]. These interaction plays out different depending on the agenda. Oftentimes interactions on social media are of political agenda [Fer+16], are so-called political social bots[2] are used for a variety of benign and malicious purposes, though the latter have understandably received some attention. A recent paper [Fer+16] defines political social bots as automated scripts designed to influence public opinion. The authors point out that political bots have been used for various purposes, including to spread misinformation, inflate the visibility of political actors or issues, or spread fake news simply to create an environment of informational uncertainty.

Researchers at University of California do also come to such conclusion [Fer+16] and have found that during political discussions regarding the 2016 US presidential election approximately 15 percent of the users participating were bots. These bots were responsible for around 19 percent of overall conversations. And it does not stop there, political social bots have played a key role in several political elections and referendums. During the Brexit referendum in the United Kingdom, they manipulated public opinion in favor of the country to leave the European Union [Bir19]. Bots also interfered with the French presidential elections in 2017 by spreading the MacronLeaks campaign against Emmanuel Macron [Fer17]. Bots actively shape public opinion, usually by negative campaigning [Bir19] and influence individuals who may not be able to distinguish between human or bot generated content. As a consequence, much research effort has been put into the classification and detection of social bots. These efforts ranges from deep neural network models [KF18] to supervised learning algorithms [HM16]. Yet, it is still unclear how easy an average online social media user can implement social bots, which platforms they target, where they originate from, how sophisticated these bots are and what capabilities that are required to implement one.

What is clear, however, is that social bots need a technical infrastructure, which can be broadly understood as the combination of (1) the profile on a social media platform and (2) the technical preconditions for partial automation of the account's behavior through the accordant platform's Application Programming Interface [Ass+20]. This infrastructure has become available for the public and one can ask if the capabilities required to implement a social bot has due to the availability of these

---

[1] the internet where websites emphasize user-generated content

[2] Same as social bots but aims to spread information with political content

resources become more manageable. Therefore, the question of whom is able to implement a social bot and what capabilities are required in the process is becoming increasingly more important. Why such a question is of importance through a societal perspective is to get a better understanding of which kind of people can operate these bots and which infrastructure they use to counteract these operations.

1.1 Problem

This work addresses the lack of studies done regarding the required capabilities of the person who intends to create and implement a social media bot. The problem's severity escalates with the rapid technological advancements making a potentially harmful tool available to the public. Therefore, this study aims to shed a light of what is needed to implement a social bot and what capabilities are required in the process.

1.2 Purpose

The purpose of this work is to map what is needed to implement a social bot on a social media platform and what capabilities are required in the process.

1.3 Goal

The goal of this book is to map what capabilities are required to implement a social bot, in order to understand who is able to implement one. We wish to help further studies regarding bot detection methods by delivering a base of capabilities.

1.4 Method

A qualitative research approach laid the basis for this book. The qualitative research method is well suited to gain understanding of the meaning and behaviors for developing information systems or artifacts [Håk13]. Furthermore, the qualitative research method is described as a well-suited choice for implementation-oriented studies as this one. Since an implementation of a software program was part of this study's scope, a design strategy was outlined. It started with exploratory research, where available information within desired topic was gathered and evaluated. Later it transitioned to an action research approach, where planning, action, and evaluation was essential. This method was well-suited for the following two reasons:

1. Neither of the authors have created a social media bot before, hence we needed to explore the options available.

2. A social bot had to be implemented, hence planned actions had to be taken to implement one.

1.5 Limitations and scope

This work is focused on the required capabilities to implement a social bot on a social media platform. Since there are numerous different social media platforms available on the market today, the scope for this book was limited to utilize the social platform Twitter. Twitter was chosen because it's one of the largest platforms and because politics is a widely discussed topic on the platform. The scope was limited to one platform to be able to carry out a more thorough and delimited study.

Since there are multiple resources to implement a bot available on the internet, we had to choose one to utilize. Twitter offers a development portal with tools, one of them being used to create and implement a bot. However, since the scope of this study was to map capabilities, the study did not investigate how the implemented bot interacted in its environment.

Another constraint was the fact that the subjects of this book were the authors themselves. This led to the capabilities being assessed were based on the authors competencies and experiences. Since the authors were students within Information and Communication Technology at the Royal Institute of Technology (KTH) both had years of experience of programming and other computing competence.

With this in mind the scope for the study was limited to assess the capabilities and tools necessary for a person of a similar background to implement a social bot.

1.5.1 Target group

This work is mainly aimed at two target groups, industry, and academia. For academia, the work presents a new way of approaching bots and what is required to implement one. Hopefully, this will contribute to a new basis within bot-detection methods and preventing malicious intent from spreading. For the industry, the work can shed a light on the availability for bot implementation technology. Since large technology companies like Twitter or Meta has major challenges with bots and misinformation this can hopefully shed a light on who can implement a bot for new discussions to take place regarding user policies of the availability of bot implementation resources.

1.6   Benefits, Ethics and Sustainability

In conjunction with the goal of this work, we wished to contribute with mapping of which capabilities that are required to implement a bot on a social platform. The social benefits of this will hopefully be a new way of approaching the challenges with bots and the spreading of malicious intent. This approach could be benefiting for anyone who wish to develop bot detection technologies.

Although Twitter do not restrict the use of bots, they are often created to steal data or limit free speech [SB18]. These actions break laws and are of essential threats to human rights; and can thus be considered unethical. The ethics we wish to be obeyed in this study was to help counteract this and for our own implemented bot ensure that no harm was done.

This book touches on social sustainability. Since social sustainability is a process for creating sustainable places that promote wellbeing. With our result we wish to contribute to healthier and a more sustainable climate on the social media platforms.

1.7   Outline

The remainder of the book is structured as follows:

2 Theoretical Background: In this chapter, we take a closer look at the theory and background that is relevant to our project.

3 Research Method: This chapter explains the methods, approached strategies as well as research phases performed during this book.

4 Implementation: In this chapter, we present basic needs that were fundamental in the implementation of the bot. Also, a wide description of selected capabilities which we assumed were required are described.

5 Results: This chapter presents the results from the implementation, a step-by-step guide will be outlined and corresponding capabilities that were needed.

6 Analysis: This chapter analyzes the comparisons and results from the previous chapter deeper.

7 Discussion: Here, all information and analyzed results are interpreted as found by us during the book and our own thoughts are presented.

8 Conclusion and Future Work: In this chapter we discuss what conclusions can be drawn from the book results and possible future work that can build on this book.

2 Theoretical Background

This chapter describes the theoretical concepts touched in this work. It's divided into three main sections covering *Social Networks*, *Bots* and *Technology*. Section 2.1 and 2.1.1 introduces social media networks, especially Twitter, and its issues, followed by section 2.1.2 and 2.1.3 where the concept of fake news disseminated on these media and its impact on society is described. Section 2.2 presents a description of bots, what they are, how they work and in what different ways they are designed. Section 2.2.1 and 2.2.2 takes a closer look at one of these designs, so called social bots and how they actively engage in social media. Section 2.3 covers the more technical part which underlies this study. It presents some key concepts that a computer enables, such as integrated developing environment (IDE), an application programming interface (API). Finally, section 2.4 presents an overview of what can be seen as capabilities within a software development perspective.

2.1 The Social Networks

A social network or social media is a computer-based technology that facilitates communication, sharing of ideas, thoughts, and information through virtual networks with just the press of a button [Dol21]. Social media is an online internet-based service which offers its user fast available communication of different content, such as text, videos, or photos. Since social media is internet based, users engage through smartphones, computers, or other devices with internet access. New statistics shows that there are 4.65 billion people worldwide that uses social media [Kem22]. The ability to reach large crowds at low cost is being seen as an asset and an opportunity for businesses. Companies use the platform to find and engage with customers, drive sales through advertising and promotion, gauge consumer trends, and offer customer service or support [Dol21].

The rise of social media with its commercial penalties through online advertisement has changed the way people communicate, perceive, and share information [Dol21]. Its availability and demand is continuously growing and there is almost a platform for anyone, regardless of its purpose [Wet19]. The biggest platforms today are Facebook (2.74 billion users), YouTube (2.29 billion users), WhatsApp (2 billion users) and Instagram (1.22 billion users) [Dol21]. Social media has entered and taken over the fine room where political conversations are being held. One such platform is Twitter, which politicians utilize to engage and reach potential voters [Jun14].

2.1.1 Twitter

Twitter is a global social media platform that provides human social networking services and is one of the world's biggest social platforms. Currently there are 396.5 million total users where 229 million are active daily [Sta22]. Twitter is categorized as a micro-blogging service since it has limited the number of characters one can use to 280 when forming posts, also called tweets (small messages) [OM11]. This adjustment has made the tweets easy to read and write and has created a climate like emails or blogs since members can share their ideas and experiences fast with any other user on the platform. Users can like, share (re-tweet), post (tweet) and follow other users on the platform which invites an open discussion between users [PM14]. Each user has their own personalized timeline where their tweets are assembled. When someone starts following another user (such as a friend, company, or celebrity), a stream of the followed user's content will be shown.

Twitter is not just an ordinary social media platform where people share their ideas and opinions, it has developed to a key real time communication channel for news during disasters and political events [OM11]. Due to the efficient, simultaneous communication tool which Twitter is, it has become a commonly used communication platform for politicians. On Twitter politicians can promote their campaigns, have direct conversations with voters, mobilize their supporters, and influence the public agenda [SS18]. This was extra clear during the 2016 US presidential election day when more than 75 million tweets were posted and most of them had a political agenda [SS18].

This participation and engagement from the public (where, for many social media has become their main source of news), spreading of misinformation also called fake news has become a tool for polarization and a real threat against society [DB18]. Studies has shown that between one out of three news stories published on Twitter from known publishers was of fake content during the early stages of the 2016 US election [AG17]. Another study showed that misinformation on Twitter is more likely to be retweeted by people, and far more rapidly, than true information, especially when the topic is politics [AT19].

2.1.2 Fake news

Fake news (FN) has become a widely controversial term, used in many different contexts. Media matters [DB18] defines FN as false or misleading information that is clearly demonstrably fabricated, presented and distributed as news. FN has been around for centuries but had a significant surge during the 2016 US presidential election. During the campaign, republican Donald Trump accused the American news channels CNN, NBC, ABC for actively disseminate fake news. This led to people questioning science, true news (TN), and societal norms [Ald17]. FN is increasingly affecting societal values, changing opinions on critical issues and topics as well as redefining facts, truths, and beliefs [Ald17].

The concept of fake news is not something new, it has been around since the early age of human civilization [DB18]. Prominent in various forms like hoaxes, rumors, and propaganda [DB18]. It has been used as a tool to gain power and manipulate civilizations for bad and for good. With the rise of social media and web 2.0 where users of the internet have a central role in content creation. Content can be created anonymously and published without excessive examination for validity and authenticity [DB18]. This is especially so when the content touches controversial or emotionally charged topics. The emotional reactions of users contribute to the fast pace at which information spreads, and the sheer volume of information that people are now subjected to makes it very difficult to assess truthfulness [Wet19].

2.1.3 Societal impact

Fake news has led to an increased concern due to it is impact on democratic systems [DB18]. In the aftermath of several fake news stories going viral, researchers speculated how these stories might have had an impact on voters in the 2016 US election [AG17]. There are tangible reasons for this concern. Recent surveys show that social media is the primary news source for 62 percent of US adults [GS16]. Furthermore, a large proportion of people who see the fake news claim that they believe them [AG17].

Fake news is not just related to the United States, it is a global issue. For instance, a study done by the *Swedish Defense Research Agency* and *Oxford university* regarding the 2018 election in Sweden showed that Swedish social media users were sharing a vast amount fake news. One out of every three news stories being shared with political hashtags was of fake content, the largest proportion of all the European elections studied [Hed+18].

2.2 Bots

Bots, agents, or actors are applications that can execute predefined tasks and do so repetitively. It is a software agent executed by computers without needing human control [GG18]. A bot is a piece of executable software that automates the process of interaction between users and content or other users [RW18].

Bots have been around since the early age of automation. One of the first types of automated programs were chatbots [3]. Chatbots became popular in the 90's due to the increased participation in online chat rooms. Bot functions within these platforms were, among other things, to warn users if they used inappropriate language in the chat and exclude people who expressed inappropriate language. A more advanced chatbot is a chatterbot[4], where the bot can respond to messages and have a profound discussion with the writer, which means that from the writer's perspective, the bot can appear as human [Bir19].

The chatterbot has become a widely used tool for companies as it is an efficient tool for automation of processes contributing to 24/7 services [GG18]. The availability and capacity these bots generate has resulted in several advancements[5]:

Cost savings for companies.

Faster internal processes.

Reaching new customers through social media platforms.

Gather a deeper understanding of customers behaviour and personalize interaction.

A 24/7 availability for customer service with multilingual conversations with instant reply.

Apart from chatterbots, bots have a widely range of usage areas and can be embodied in many ways. Gorwa and Guilbeault [GG18] have researched on bots and claim that the main six different types of bots are:

Web Robots: Automated scripts that acts in the web, deployed to download, and index webpages in large quantities.

Chatterbot: Programs that approximate human speech and interact with humans directly through some sort of interface. Chatterbots seek to design programs that can sustain at least basic dialogue with a human user.

Spambots: Bots that advertise and post spam on online messaging platforms.

Social bots: General concept of automation that operates on social platforms. Automated accounts disguised as real users acting on social media platforms.

Sock Puppets and trolls: User accounts assuming the identity of others.

Cyborgs and hybrid accounts: A combination of automated and human supervision.

The purpose of this study is focused primarily on the type of bot called social bot; this type of bot will be described in more detail in the next section.

2.2.1   Social bots

Social media bots are special types of bots which act as humans. They are hidden behind social media accounts interacting with humans and influencing them with political, ideological, or commercial purposes [ED19]. The complexity of the bot varies in relation to the level of automation and can be seen as Semi-automated or Automated.

Semi-automated social media bots allow a user to program a set of parameters but may have or require additional user interaction or a greater degree of management. These types of social media bots are typically fake accounts with fake personalities and are run at least partially by humans, rather than a programming language [ca18].

Automated social media bots allow the user to establish a set of parameters using programming language within an application. The automation can be done through e.g., hashtag every time a message is posted, but not when the bot itself share it, which the social media bot then executes without human interaction [ca18].

The United States Department of Homeland Security has mapped common attack methods by social bots [ca18]:

> Click Farming or Like Farming: infiltrate popularity or fame through liking or re-posting of content via click farms, which provide fake user accounts (typically semi-automated social media bots) and management of the social media bots for purchase.
>
> Hashtag Hijacking: use hashtags to focus an attack (e.g., spam, malicious links) on a specific audience using common hashtags.
>
> Repost Storm: use a parent social media bot account, or martyr social media bot, to initiate an attack by re-posting something, which an associated group of social media bots instantly repost.
>
> Trend Jacking and Watering Hole Attack: use top trending topics to focus on an intended audience for targeting purposes.

According to a research report made by Oxford Internet Institute [Hed+18], the influence of social bots on mainstream social media in the United States, Russia, Germany, Canada, China, and other countries cannot be underestimated [Hed+18]. Social bots, as a computer program, can control social accounts, automatically post messages on social platforms, and use relevant technologies such as artificial intelligence to mimic and interact with human users. At present, social media platforms such as Twitter and Facebook have found more and more social bots, which has profoundly affected many fields such as economy, politics, and people's social life [Fer+16]. And it has been proved that social bots are largely responsible for the massive spread of misinformation, which posed a major threat to democracies [Cre+15].

2.2.2 Bots on Twitter

Bots have become a significant part of the interactions being held and content spread on Twitter [Bir19]. A consequence of this is the uncertainty regarding which accounts are bot and not. A study which investigated 716 randomly selected Twitter profiles categorized users into six different classes of Twitter users [MS14]:

1. Personal users: Users who use the platform for fun, learn or read news, do not promote any business or product, and their social interactions are low or mild.

2. Professional users: Home users who have many followers and follow many. They mainly focus on one area by sharing useful information about it.

3. Business users: Users who frequently tweet but have little interactions. Their behavior follows a similar pattern to each other, following a marketing and business strategy.

4. Spam users: Randomly follow users and spread malicious tweets, their behavior follows the same pattern to each other.

5. Feed and News: These accounts post news-related tweets. They are not interactive with other users.

6. Viral and Marketing Services: Accounts that serve to increase sales, brand awareness or marketing objectives.

The first three of the above-mentioned user classes belong to human accounts, whereas the last three to machines also known as digital actors or bots.

A bot acting on Twitter is a special type of account controlled by a machine rather than a human. These accounts can automatically tweet, re-tweet, like, follow, unfollow, and send direct messages. Twitter does not restrict the use of bots if they follow the automation rules[6]. Bots can broadcast helpful information, respond to users in direct messages or try new solutions which help people. On the other hand, bots are not supposed to spam, spread misinformation, or violate any other policies [Cre+15]. However, Twitter bots are like regular bots, they can be benign, broadcasting news and helpful information, but they can also be harmful, spreading misinformation and promoting hate speech [Cre+15].

A study done by Stanford University [AS14] highlighted the high activity by social bots in the online political discussion of the 2016 USA presidential election. Their study showed that social bots posted nearly 3.8 million tweets accounting for one-fifth of the total. Their experiments suggested that both the Hillary Clinton and Trump teams have used social bots to conduct political propaganda on Twitter and attack the opponent. The same phenomenon of political social bots was also discovered by **47**, and they conducted an in-depth analysis of these bots' media articles. Hence the analysis of social bots can help control the spread of harmful information.

2.3 Software development

This section describes high level technical aspects to understand how a computer works.

2.3.1 Compiler

A compiler is the core for translation within a computer, it compiles source code[7] from a higher-level programming language to a low-level programming language [IBM20].

2.3.2 A low-level programming language

Low-level usually refers to machine code or assembly languages, simple instruction but are considered to be more difficult to use, the simplicity and difficulty comes with an upside, no compiler is needed, and the programmer has full control and the ability to write more efficient code[8].

2.3.3 A high-level programming language

High-level refers to languages that are commonly used by programmers. Ranging from C, C++, to Java, JavaScript and Python. They are distinguishing form low-level languages since they depend on a compiler or an interpreter to translate the language used into machine code. efficiency[9].

2.3.4 Integrated development environment

An integrated development environment (IDE) is a tool for software developers. It is a software application designed to maximize the developer's productivity and increase the developer's experience[10]. This enhanced experience is possible by combining common activities of writing software into a single application such as, intelligent source code editing, building executables and debugging.

IDEs are used to simplify code development. One popular IDE is Visual studio code, and it has a large section of extensions. An extension can be coloring syntax, spelling correction or code suggestion and are all examples of source code editing.

2.3.5   Application programming interface

An application programming interface, or more commonly known by its acronym API, is a tool for applications to communicate with other applications, a software intermediary that enables applications to exchange data and functionality easily and securely [IBM20].

An API enables connections between computers or pieces of software to each other. It is often made up of different parts which act as tools or services that are available to the programmer. A program or that uses one of these parts is said to call that portion of the API. The calls can be seen as instructions and are also known as subroutines, methods, requests, or endpoints[11]. An instruction could be everything from verifying credentials to liking someone's twitter post or even post your own. Some APIS have rules require access credentials, amount of time allowed to access and country of origin. In many cases this is well documented and a necessity if anyone that is not the creator of the API is to use it.

2.3.6   Server

A server is an ordinary computer on a network with a specific task. The task is to serve other computers on the network with its service. The computers asking for service are called clients and the relation between the two creates a client-server model. A single server can serve multiple clients, and a single client can use multiple servers. There are several types of servers and therefore many types of services although usually each server is dedicated to one e.g., mail, web, file, or database[11].

2.3.7   Database and Cloud server

Database: A database is an organized collection of structured data that is typically stored electronically in a computer system. A database is usually controlled by a database management system (DBMS) which is the software that interacts with end users, applications, and the database itself to capture and analyze the data. Together, the data and the DBMS, along with the applications that are associated with them, are referred to as a database system, often shortened to just database[12].

Through the organized and structured data, databases provide efficient processing and querying of the data. The data can then be easily accessed, managed, modified, updated, controlled, and organized. Most databases use structured query language (SQL) for writing and querying data.

Cloud server: A cloud server or cloud computing is a service provided through the internet including servers, storage, databases, networking, analytics, software, and intelligence. Cloud services provides its customers with IT infrastructure or data centers, companies can rent access to anything from applications to storage from a cloud service provider. This provides faster innovation, flexible resources, and economies of scale[13].

There are five main services on the market today [Dig21]:

1. Amazon Web Services (AWS) which dominate with one third of market shares

2. Microsoft Azure

3. Google Cloud Platfrom

4. Alibaba Cloud

5. IBM

2.4   Capabilities within software engineering

To be able to develop software systems and launch programs on the internet several capabilities linked to software engineering are required. As a software developer, capabilities are associated with the ability to (1) *Analyze* concepts, problems and identify appropriate high-level solutions. To be able to (2) *Develop* well designed software systems and (3) *Test* and evaluate these systems [Gro18].

Since the field of software development is very wide and it is a matter of taste over what capabilities a software developer needs, many organizations have tried to research this. One of them is the Object Management Group[14] (OMG). OMG is a non-profit technological consortium[15] founded in 1998 with an international, open-membership approach and are specialized in software development standards. More specifically, they provide specifications of object models with data and methods. One of these specifications focuses on language for and software development, where they in detail describes competences within a software development perspective. They describe a competency as" encompasses *the abilities, capabilities, attainments, knowledge, and skills necessary to do a certain kind of work"* [Gro18]. In more detail OMG describes (1) *Analysis*, (2) *Development* and (3) *Testing* as:

1. *Analysis*: The competency to analyze is the deductive ability to understand the situation, context, concepts, and problems, identify appropriate high-level solutions, and evaluate and draw conclusions by applying logical thinking [Gro18].

   When developing software, it is essential that the current situation is analyzed, and the correct requirements identified for the new system. The requirements themselves must also be analyzed to make sure that they are, among other things, practical, achievable, and appropriately sized to drive the system's development. The analysis competency encapsulates the abilities needed to successfully define the system to be built.

2. *Development/software development*: The competency to develop systems encapsulates the ability to design and program effective software systems following the standards and norms as the task requires. More specific, development competency is the mental ability to conceive and produce a software system, or one of its elements, for a specific function or task. It enables one to produce software systems that meet the requirements. The development competency is about solving complex problems and producing effective software systems. It lies in the observing, the sensemaking of, and representing the system as others expect it to see it, that is, as effective and functional and easy to use. All this in turn requires the ability to imagine and visualize code and structure it in a way so that it is easy to understand and maintain [Gro18].

3. *Testing*: The competency and the ability to test a system, verifying that it is usable, and that it meets the requirements. The testing competency is an observational, comparative, detective, and destructive ability that enables the system to be tested. To test that the system meets the requirements and demonstrate that it is fit for purpose is essential when developing software. The ability to conceive and undertake testing is essential throughout the evolution of a system and is an essential complement to the tasks design and programming capabilities [Gro18].

3   Research Method

This chapter introduces and describes the research method used in this study. An overview of performed research strategy will be presented in section 3.1 to establish a strategy for the study. In section 3.2 a division of performed phases is presented. Section 3.3 introduces chosen research methods and section 3.4 describes the different research instruments. Finally, section 3.5 and 3.6 evaluates and motivates validity threats and ethical requirements to ensure that the study is reliable.

3.1   Research strategies

The research area covered int this study (regarding social bots) is a wide and relatively unexplored area. To optimize the study, a research strategy was chosen that could streamline implementation. The research phases consist of the initial steps that were made in the research process to facilitate the understanding of the research instruments used in the study (to gain required knowledge to implement a social bot). Then the research method was chosen that was best suited to treat the research instruments. Finally, validity threats and ethical requirements were established to evaluate the research method. Figure 1 presents the five key factors of the strategy: (1) *research phases*, (2) *research methods*, (3) *research instruments*, (4) *validity threats* and (5) *ethical requirements*.

Figure 1: illustrates the five components of the research strategy.

3.2   Methods

The following section describes and motivates for the research approach and methodology used in this project. First, in section 3.3.1 we compare the qualitative and quantitative research approach. Then, in section 3.3.2 we motivate for the chosen design strategy's *Exploratory research* and *Action research*. There are many different methodologies to use in a project and there are different cases where some are more appropriate than others.

3.2.1   Qualitative research method

In accordance with the nature of the study, two different research methods were utilized. One for each part of the study, first a qualitative approach for the evolution of the selected *capabilities* suitable for different skill levels. The qualitative method gave the study the opportunity to interpret and break down the documents and data used in the practical part of the study where all documents, facts, and theory where reviewed and evaluated.

The qualitative Research method concerns understanding meanings, opinions, and behaviors to reach tentative hypotheses and theories. It is suitable to develop computer systems, artifacts, and inventions. The method commonly uses smaller data sets that are sufficient to reach reliable results [Håk13].

A qualitative methodology was utilized because the study did not have a large enough scale. The study did not generate enough data to justify the use of a quantitative analysis, it was utilized to understand a certain topic (technology behind social bots) to develop a software system (implementation of social bot).

Quantitative Research method support experiments and testing by measuring variables to verify or falsify theories and hypothesis. The formation of the hypothesis is that it must be measurable and quantifiable. The method requires large data sets and use statistics to test the hypothesis and make the research project valid. [Håk13] A quantitative approach was not appropriate for this study, it had too small scale and too little data was generated. A quantitative approach could have been executed if we would start gather data from our bot which then would be analyzed.

3.2.2   Exploratory and Action Research

For the second part of the study a combination of the methodology's *Action research* and *Exploratory research* was utilized. Both were performed when implementing the social bot. Action research was of benefit when acting, testing, and evaluating the bot while the exploratory research was done within the design phase of the substrate for the bot and capabilities.

Action research [Avi+99] is performed by taking actions in a systematic and cyclic way. It contributes to an open research approach by combining practice and theory. The method improves the way people address issues and solves problems, as well as strategies, practices, and knowledge of environments. Figure 2 demonstrates the cyclic behavior of the method, where planning, action, evaluation, and reflection are essential. Action research often studies communities or settings with restricted data sets and, hence, qualitative methods are most suitable [Håk13].

Action research was utilized because of this research attempt to contribute to practical concerns in problematic situations. This research has the potential to change the way corporations and people address issues, that is, to change their way of thinking and approaching ethical and available APIs for developing bots as well as shape methods to counteract malicious acts from these bots.

The exploratory research method has a purpose to provide a basis when exploring general findings, the possibility to obtain as many relationships between different variables as possible [Dud12]. This design approach was a guideline through the preparation phase for the implementation of the bot.

Also, exploratory research uses surveys to get an insight into the problem. It rarely provides definite answers to specific issues. Instead, it identifies key issues and variables to define objectives, using qualitative data collection [Håk13]. In our study exploratory research was used during the design phase, gathering information and sources to utilize during the implementation of the bot as well as developing required capabilities.

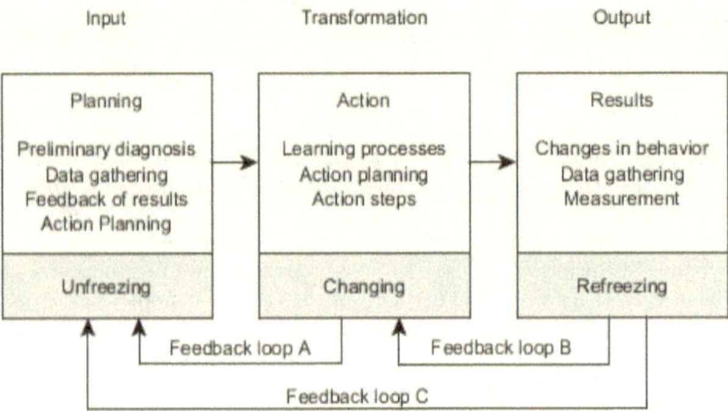

Figure 2: Illustration of action research

3.3   Research phases

The study was divided and mainly executed within five different phases. Phase one was a pre-phase consisting of a literature in combination with a practical study where arbitrary information was gathered to proceed into the next phase of the study. Phase two (Preparation and design) used the gathered information from phase one to prepare and design the technical processes and select the required capabilities. Phase three covered the implementation of the social bot, phase four consisted of evaluating given results from past phases (two and four). Given result, adjustments and improvements were made in an iterative process between phase two, three and four. Finally phase five focused on analysis. This way of conducting the feasibility study meant that sufficient prior knowledge of the work could be met before the study began. These phases are illustrated in Figure 3.

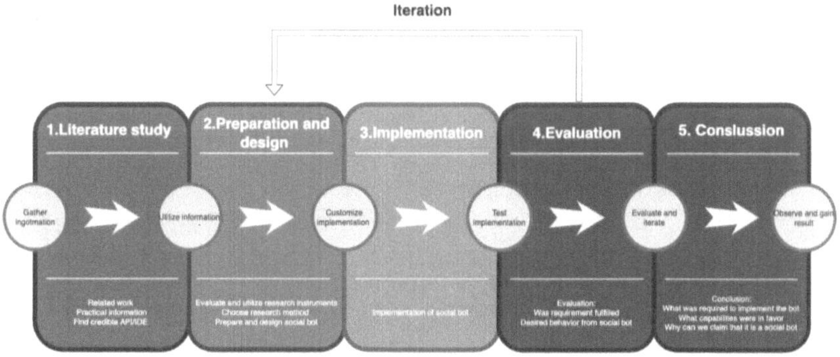

Figure 3: Visual representation of the executed phases

3.3.1 Literature and practical study

The literature study phase was executed through an *exploitative research* approach, focused to provide a background of facts regarding social bots and capabilities required to implement one. Non-fiction literature as *Essence – Kernel and Language for Software Engineering Methods* [Gro18] was used to provide both credible and relevant basics when developing/forming capabilities. Also, academical search engines such as Google Scholar [GOO22], ScienceDirect [Sci22] and DiVA [DiV22] were utilized. Searches via selected keywords such as: *social bots*, *bots*, *bots on twitter*, *bots*, *malicious intent*, and *implementation of bots* resulted in thousands of articles and papers. Out of these a few were selected, some articles were of related work/findings and some gave theoretical explanations within desired topics. Figure 4 presents the first phase.

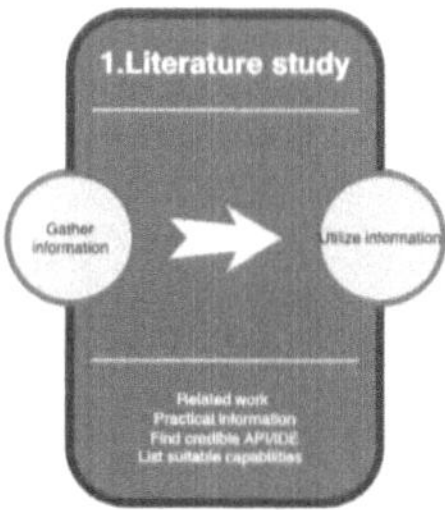

Figure 4: Phase one, literature and practical study

In parallel with the literature study a practical study was performed. The literature study focused on theoretical background and information as a basis for the project's theoretical structure, where our practical study focused on state of practice. In other words, available, open-source applications that performs social bot implementations on the web. We found that modern companies already today contributed to highly sophisticated software applications.

3.3.2 Preparation and design

Based on the findings from phase one, preparations via available platforms and design via open source where made. The preparations required some kind of evaluation, hence evaluation criteria with a *qualitative approach* were constructed (see section 3.4.3). This model was both part of the preparation process and the evaluation process (after the bot was implemented). To have an evaluation model to follow was a helpful guideline, both when selecting capabilities and when testing the bot. Regarding the bot, the model was for the purpose of ensuring that a social bot had been implemented. Another model for evaluating what could be seen as capabilities was for the purpose of ensuring that suitable capabilities had been selected.

Further preparations were utilized regarding available APIS (Application Program Interface) and IDE (Integrated Development Environment) for Twitter development options. Many accessible guides where available, which brought the practical approach as the next step to be taken. Figure 5 presents the second phase.

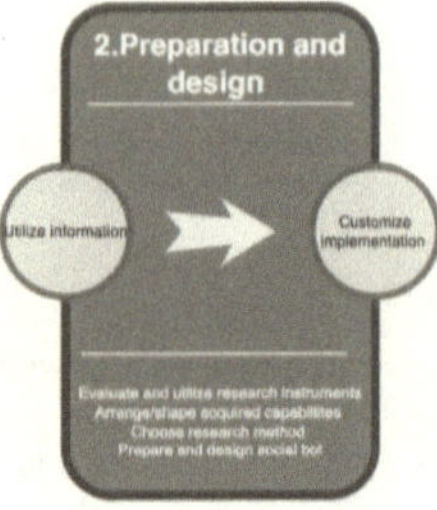

Figure 5: Phase two, preparation and design

3.3.3 Implementation

From gained knowledge and the preparation process, actions were taken through an attempt to implement a social bot on Twitter (each step in the process was documented and is presented in more detail in the result section 5.2). Actions taken was based to sustain an *action research* approach. After the implementation, suitable capabilities were developed and selected with the intention to be linked to the specific step in the implementation process where they were required. Figure 6 presents the third phase.

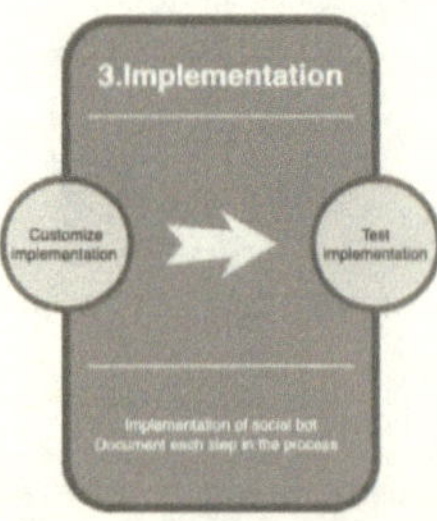

Figure 6: Phase three, Implementation

3.3.4   Evaluation

Since we ourselves had to objectively judge the implemented bot and at the same time be as non-bias as possible, we had to explore what capabilities we hold from a third person perspective. To judge yourself in an evaluative manner were perceived unfit and addressed in the section 3.5 Validity threats. A capability is classified as the smallest domain of knowledge area.

As many assumptions had to be made, evaluation was essential. Both to evaluate if the bot was considered a social bot (which could integrate and function on Twitter) but also to select suitable capabilities that were required through the process. If the bot was not functioning as planned, we had to look back to phase two, reflect on what went wrong, adjust errors, and try again. This process was part of the *action research* agenda, which contributed to productivity and enhanced the validity and credibility of the study. Evaluation was based on different criteria introduced in section 3.4.2. Figure 7 presents the fourth phase.

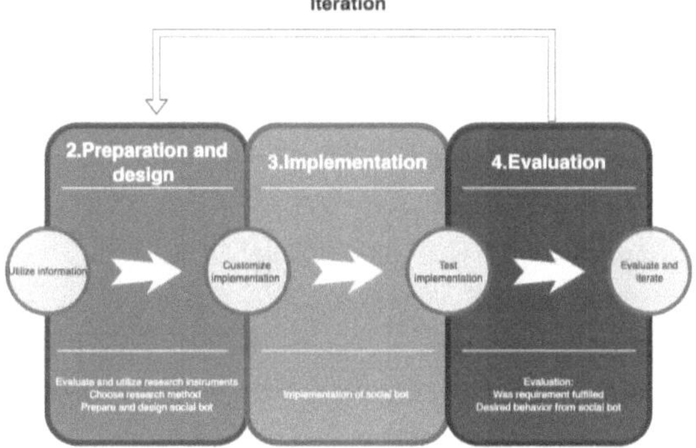

Figure 7: Phase four, Evaluation process

3.3.5.   Conclusion

The last phase of the study was to analyze and reflect the gained results from the process. Each executed step from the implementation of the bot had to be considered as well as the final bot itself. From this knowledge we had to conclude and demonstrate the required capabilities for each step. Figure 8 presents the fourth phase.

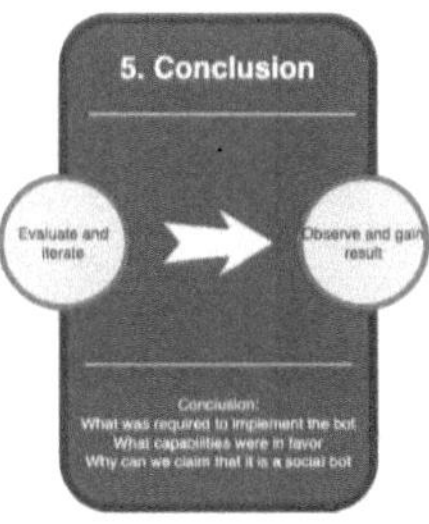

Figure 8: Phase five, Conclusion

3.4   Research instruments

This section presents and describes used research instruments. This to ensure that the instruments used in the study are adequately used and suitable for the research methods.

3.4.1   Moscow model

The Moscow model is a strategic prioritization methodology model that arranges importance on different aspects, but mostly it requires you to reflect on potential choices [Bru20]. Why such instrument was of interest for this study is because many assumptions had to be made when categorizing the implemented bot as social. This makes a prioritization model very appropriate, where assumptions must be motivated and evaluated. Moscow is short for: **M**ust have, **S**hould have, **C**ould have and **W**on't have. Below, several requirements are categorized within each step acting as criteria which the bot should fulfill.

1. **Must have** (what must be included): A social bot must have the ability to [GG18]:

   Profile: Have a profile of some representation

   Follow: Follow user accounts

   Follow back: Able to follow and unfollow other users who start follow the bot

   Retweet: Share other users content

   Add Tweet: Create basic own topics and share content

   Follow tweet: Follow content of specific topics

   Quote: Quote other users statements

   Use hashtags: Utilize hashtags to find desired topics

2. **Should have** (what should be included): A social bot should have the ability to:

   Send direct message to user: Can be text based, videos or pictures

   Send direct message to followers: Can be text based, videos or pictures

   Followers to list: Add followers to a list

   Public reply: Comment on other user's content

3. **Could have** (what could be included): A social bot could have the ability to:

   Tweets lookup: Search for specific tweets

   Manage Tweets: Manage to create own content and share in the timeline.

   Timelines: Adjust frequency of which content is spread, specific timelines when it should act

   Search Tweets: Search for specific tweet

   Tweet counts: Keep track of data and chose how many tweets to share.

   Filtered stream: Filter stream of specific content, utilize hashtags

4. **Won't have** (not to be included): A social bot (in our case) will not have the ability to:

   Act on other platforms

   Share malicious intent

   Interact with other users to collect personal information

   Spam specific users

3.4.2   Evaluation criteria

To ensure that the selected capabilities were suitable, and that the implementation of the bot was reliable, several criteria had to be considered. These criteria was the set of principles or standards by which judgement was made [LM99]. Hence, an evaluation model had to be constructed and followed.

We followed the Object Management Group [Gro18] approach regarding competencies and capabilities, of what they call" a *sequence of competency levels ranging from a minimum level of competency to a maximum level"*. Typically, the levels range from 1–*Beginner* to 5–*innovates*. These five competency levels define:

1. Beginner:

    Demonstrates a basic understanding of the concepts and can follow instructions.

    The following describe the traits of a Level 1 individual:

    Can correctly respond to basic task and concept within his or her domain.

    Can perform most basic functions within the domain.

    Can follow instructions and complete basic tasks.

2. Experienced:

    Able to apply the concepts in simple contexts by routinely applying the experience gained so far.

    The following describe the traits of a Level 2 individual:

    Can collaborate with others to create systems.

    Can satisfy routine demands and do simple work requirements.

    Can handle simple challenges with confidence.

    Can handle simple work requirements but needs help in handling any complications or difficulties.

    Can reason about the context and draw sensible conclusions.

3. Adaptive

    Able to adapt and apply the concepts in various contexts and has the experience to work without supervision.

    The following describe the traits of a Level 3 individual:

    Can satisfy most demands and work requirements.

    Can utilize the language of the competency's domain with ease and accuracy.

    Can communicate and explain his or her work.

    Knows the limits of his or her capability and when to call on more expert advice.

    Works at a professional level with little or no guidance.

4. Masters

    Able to apply judgment on when and how to apply the concepts to more complex contexts. Can enable others to apply the concepts

    The following describe the traits of a Level 4 individual:

    Can satisfy complex demands and work requirements.

    Can communicate with others working outside the domain.

    Can direct and help others working within the domain.

    Can adapt his or her way-of-working to work well with others, both inside and outside their domain.

5. Innovates:

> A recognized expert, able to extend the concepts to new contexts and inspire others.

> The following describe the traits of a Level 5 individual:
>> Has many years of experience and is currently up to date in what is happening within the domain.
>> Is recognized as an expert int the field.
>> Supports others in working on complex problems.
>> Knows when to innovate or do something different and when to follow normal procedure.
>> Develops innovative and effective solutions to the current challenges within the domain.

3.4.3   Twitter development portal

For its users, Twitter offers a development portal[16] where user can apply for a development account and get access to their portal. In this portal the user gets access to the API keys[17] and endpoints for several different tasks. Such task can be to analyze user data, growth rate of users and tweets. There are three different tiers of the Twitter API but for this study the most basic one called *essential* was sufficient. *Elevated* and *Academic Research* required an application to be approved manually but came with a larger pool of API credits to use for free.

3.4.4   Software development

In the design and implementation phase of the study, python3 together with Node.js were used for communication with the server. Furthermore, Visual studio code[19] was suitable as IDE with some built in extensions. Accessible programming structures were utilized when writing the code and several python libraries: Tweepy and Pandas.

3.5   Validity threats

Validity, or trustworthiness can be seen as a quality assurance for the study, a validation and verification of the research material [Håk13]. This quality assurance in qualitative research makes sure that the research has been conducted according to some specific criteria. These criteria are based on [JD13]: (1) *Credibility*, (2) *Transferability*, (3) *Dependability* and (4) *Conformability*.
In our case since we implemented a software environment and construct different levels of capabilities, these criteria are essential to its trustworthiness and quality.

1. *Credibility*: This criterion focuses on the trustworthiness and reliability of the study. This to ensure that the produced results/findings are believable by others. To bring this about, the pre-study and study needs to be done clearly.

2. *Transferability*: In accordance with the nature of a qualitative study, transferability means that the results provided can be applied or transferred to other studies in different settings. To ensure this, a clear description of the context of which the study was conducted [JD13].

3. *Dependability*: This criterion evaluates if the research and its findings can be repeated by other scientists. Which provides if the findings are consistent in the relation to the context of which they were generated.

4. *Conformability*: This criterion is set to ensure that the study is done objective, neutral and not based on the researcher's biases and interest.

3.6 Ethical requirements

To conduct research, one must follow a form of ethical guideline, through which the research stays within social and moral values. To ensure that this research was executed within such values, several ethical requirements had to be considered. Since our research focused on an active software agent such as a bot these requirements were based on eight guidelines: (1) *Transparency*, (2) *Malicious intent*, (3) *Safety*, (4) *Responsibility*, (5) *Source criticism*, (6) *Personal privacy*, (7) *Human control* and (8) *Assumptions*.

1. *Transparency*: When developing software programs such as a software agent (bot), transparency is important if the agent causes harm. Then it should be possible to ascertain why.
   This report endeavored not to act as a guide for one to implement a bot, which would be unethical and dangerous. We, the authors actively acted to maintain a balance between openness (transparency) and care.

2. *Malicious intent*: Bots can be created in a legal manner but still be unethical, hiding its identity and accelerate the spreading of fake news is a common case [ca18]. To ensure that this would not take place, limitations were implemented, as a way of controlling the bot. It was behaving within fixed parameters.

3. *Safety*: The created bot will under no circumstances cause anyone harm or put anyone in danger. We the authors put extra thought into what type of information could be considered a *white lie*, a lie that is trivial and harmless [Pre22] and still fill the requirements needed for the project's outcome, there is a risk to benefit ratio to be considered.

4. *Responsibility*: Since we the authors of this report designed and implemented a bot which have the potential to spread information on a social platform (twitter), full responsibility of the moral implications of its use, misuse, and actions will be held.

5. *Source criticism*: Since facts and source code were retrieved from the web, source criticism was essential. To ensure that every source used was reliable and did not have a hidden agenda.

6. *Personal privacy*: Bots are most often created in an unethical manner such as steal data or limit free speech[ca18]. These actions break laws and are of essential threats to human rights. We the authors will not interact with personal users' integrity and integrate with their personal privacy.

7. *Human control*: Since the software agent (bot) acted on its own on Twitter, we the authors selected how and whether to delegate decisions made by the agent. This to accomplish humanchosen objectives.

8. *Assumptions* Each produced capability was evaluated by us the authors. Assumptions were made, considered from what we thought was suitable and reliable.

4 Implementation

This section will present the practical process and development behind selected capabilities as well as required tools for the implementation of the bot. Section 4.1 describes these tools and how they were use. Section 4.2 describes the planning behind the process followed by section 4.3 where the environment where the study was done is shown. Finally, section 4.4 presents the development behind selected capabilities, these capabilities are hypothetical.

4.1 Requirements

This section describes the different tools that were required to implement the bot. Section 4.1.1 introduces the basic needs such as a computer with internet access. Section 4.1.2 shows selected guides that were followed to implement the bot. Section 4.1.3 describes Twitters service for API access. Section 4.1.4 introduce the utilized development environment. Figure 9 illustrates a vision of the implementation process.

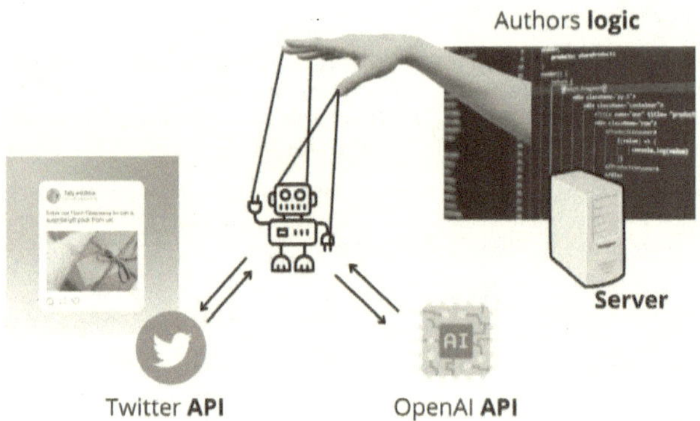

Figure 9: The vision

4.1.1 The Basics

The fundamental for this study was an environment to execute the study in *computer* and some kind of *guideline*.

Computer: A computer was needed, in this work a MacBook Pro with apple silicone (CPU/GPU).

Guideline: Guidelines was of related work where research regarding implementation of bots as [Fer+16]. Several non-scientific guidelines were available on the web, on blogs, forums. No particular guideline was strictly followed, instead they served as a base for the planning stage.

4.2 Planning

Planning was to know when each step in the guideline should be executed, this was crucial due to fact that time was an obstacle as well as our capabilities. Furthermore, we had to adapt the implementation process and which resources to utilize to ensure that the bot was a social one. Therefore, the Moscow model introduced in section 3.4.2 was checked during the process which made it easier to prioritize executed actions. These actions were purposed to fulfill what must be included for the bot to be considered social.

1. **Must have** (what must be included): A social bot must have the ability to [GG18]:

   Profile: Have a profile of some representation

   Follow: Follow user accounts

   Follow back: Able to follow and unfollow other users who start follow the bot

   Retweet: Share other users content

   Add Tweet: Create basic own topics and share content

   Follow tweet: Follow content of specific topics

   Quote: Quote other users statements

   Use hashtags: Utilize hashtags to find desired topics

4.2.1   Twitter API access

Twitter offers a specialized API service for users who wish to perform more advanced user functions[18]. This service can be accessed by applying for a developer account. For their most essential account there is only a form to be filled in, then you are granted access instantly. For this work *essential* (illustrated in figure 10) was deemed to be enough for all intents and purposes. We chose not to peruse the" *Elevated* or *Academic Research* level on the note that it required a more demanding application with approval by review.

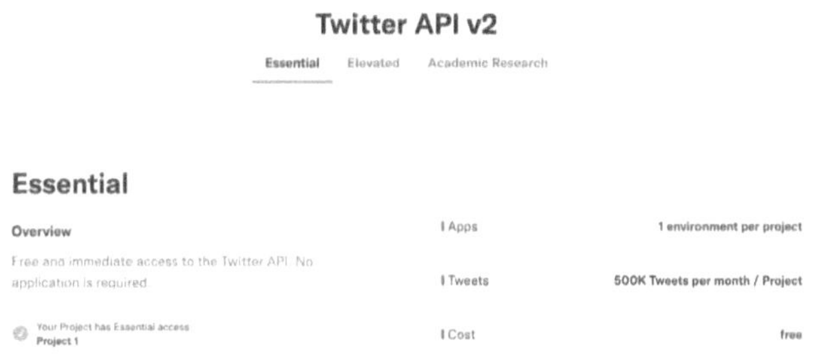

Figure 10: Twitter API v2

4.2.2   Open-AI API access

Open-AI has a range of services powered by pre-trained AI services where some are available for the public to utilize. Several of these models were suitable models for the purposes of creating an effective bot. Such as text generating models, emotion labeling or chat conversation in order to create a more advanced and human-like bot [Ope22b]. We decided to use" Tweet classifier" and" Text completion".

4.2.3   Development environment

Microsoft Visual Studio Code was used along with some extensions. The extensions were personal preferences and had no effect on the essence of the development. The programming language utilized was JavaScript (JS) and Python3 (P3), not necessarily together at once.

During the research, JS and P3 were the most common choices and had suitable library's available which purpose was to create functions for the twitter bot act on its own.

4.3   Setup

The setup for the implementation was first affected by the specific programming environment (IDE) used for the back-end server. The IDE was NodeJS, Python would have worked just as well but both authors had more experience with NodeJS which was the reason behind the choice.

The access tokens (generated from Twitter API access) for the API needed to be stored somewhere, for that *Firestore*[19] was used as a *document database*, a service within the Firebase portfolio. They could just as easily bin stored locally, the cloud was just a preference potentially to avoid future challenges if remote access would be needed.

Installation of NodeJS was a straightforward process, instructions were found on their webpage. It came with a package manager where, Firebase, Twitter, and OpenAI had available packages.

Two issues arose during the setup. The first issue was regarding the port number. Firebase tried to serve the function on port 5000 which is reserved for AirPlay on the MacOS Monterey operating system. This were resolved by turning the AirPlay off. The second issue was that the twitter API would not accept to be setup with *localhost* as the redirect address. This was solved by using the internal loop IP.

4.4   Evaluation of Capabilities

To evaluate our own capabilities objectively some kind of reliability was needed. Therefore, we proceeded to look at the courses provided by KTH that we have attended and passed. At the course webpage we looked through each course that were within *Information and Communication Technology*, the programme which the authors attend to.

This resulted in a list of capabilities (which is presented in section ??) which deemed to be useful for the implementation of the bot to have a successfully outcome.

5   Results

This section presents the study's outcome, demonstrates results and guides the reader through the implementation of the bot. Section 5.1 presents a wide range of capabilities that were required to implement the bot. Section 5.2 presents step by step the different stages performed during the implementation and which capabilities that were required in the process.

5.1   Capabilities

Seven different areas of capabilities were needed when implementing the bot, each capability consist of a capacity or knowledge required when dealing with problem solving, software development and server management. These seven areas are divided as: (1) *General*, (2) *Computer science*, (3) *Programming*, (4) *Tools*, (5) *Data transportation*, (6) *Cloud* and (7) *Math*.

1. **General**
   - Common sense
   - Problem solving
   - Analyze

2. **Computer science**
   - Algorithms
   - Data structures
   - Iteration and recursion.

3. **Programming**
   - Functional programming
   - Python 3
   - JavaScript

4. **Tools**
   - API
   - Testing
   - Analyzing (Time complexity)
   - Analyzing (Space complexity)
   - Patching

5. **Data transportation**
   - Networking
   - Communication
   - Protocols

6. **Cloud**
   - Cloud computing
   - Cloud storage
   - Cloud hosting

7. **Math**

    Discrete

    Algebra

    Statistics

    Logic

5.2   Practical implementation

This section illustrates step by step the various stages executed during the implementation of the bot and the corresponding capabilities that were required to accomplish them.

5.2.1   Step 1

The first step in creating the bot was to initialize the *cloud functions*, an emulation on local machine (computer). These functions are highlighted as green in figure 11 and were from this point accessible for any application running on the machine including the *Bot* on their endpoints. The function placed in the middle is a *callback function* and was used by accessing it via the web browser which is done in the next step.

This step required several capabilities, from programming to server management. In more detail illustrated below:

General capabilities from the second level "2. Experienced", all domains were required.

Programming capabilities on the second level "1. Beginner", all domains were required.

Cloud capabilities on the first level "1. Beginner", only cloud hosting was required from that domain.

Tools capabilities on the second level "1. Beginner", only API were required from that domain.

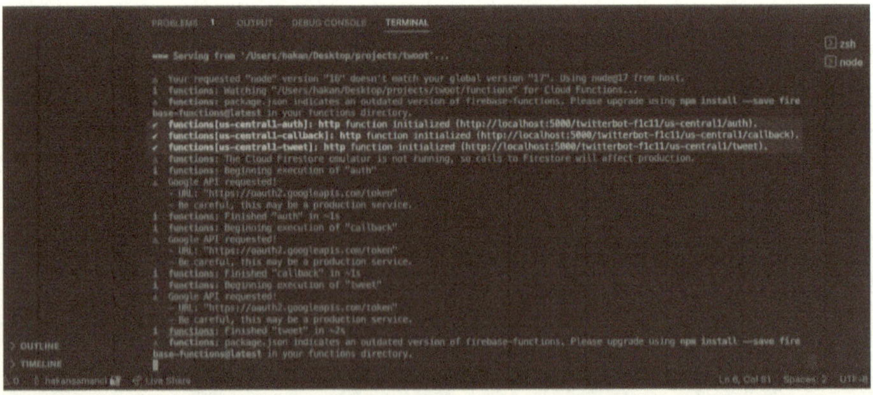

Figure 11: Highlighted in the figure, three cloud function served on with their endpoints.

5.2.2 Step 2

In step two, after the initiation of the bot an authentication was manually done to obtain the first access token and refresh token. This was done by accessing the cloud function via its uniform resource locator (URL) also called endpoint, served on the local machine. Figure 12 presents the user interface for the twitter authentication page.

This step required some programming competence and how to manage specific tools.

Programming capabilities on the second level "2. Experienced", all domains were required.

Tools capabilities on the second level "2. Experienced", only API were required from that domain.

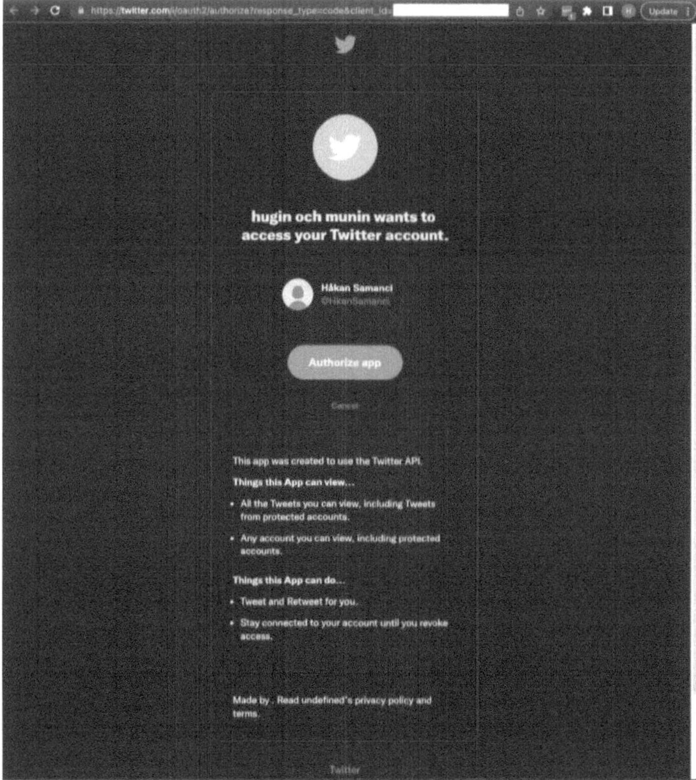

Figure 12: Twitter app authentication page

5.2.3 Step 3

In step three, after the authentication the bot had obtained its new tokens. The tokens had to be stored somewhere, we chose to save them in Firestore. Figure 13 shows an illustration of Firestore which is an open cloud (cloud server) where one can gather and store data on the web.

This step required several capabilities presented below:

General capabilities on the second level "2. Experienced", all domains were required.

Programming capabilities on the second level "2. Experienced", all domains were required.

Tools capabilities on the second level "2. Experienced", only API were required from that domain.

Cloud capabilities on the first level "1. Beginner", only cloud storage was required from that domain.

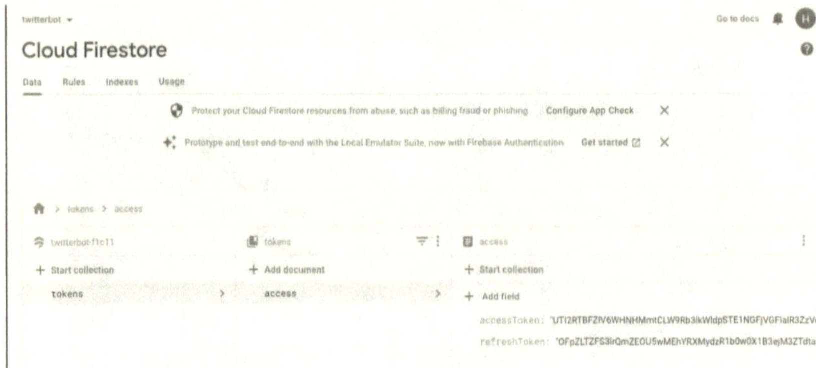

Figure 13: Tokens stored in Firestore, illustration of the user interface (UI) and the principles of a document database

5.2.4 Step 4

In step four a tweet was created by the *Bot* when it was accessing the URL endpoint called *tweet* which was initialized in step one. This function had two logical parts. The first part was to make an API call to the AI engine called *text-davinci-001* that was provided by OpenAI in order to generate the text for the tweet. The engine was provided with some information *prompt* (illustrated in figure 14). The second part was to construct and post the tweet, this was done when the first API call gets answered. The *Bot* takes the response (constructs) and makes a new call via Twitters API to post the result. This is illustrated in figure 15, where" Håkan Samanci" is the name of our bot, not the author.

```
const getTweet = await openai.createCompletion('text-davinci-001', {
  prompt: 'tweet something ridiculous #flatearth',
  max_tokens: 64,
});
```

Figure 14: Code for API call with prompt

This step required several capabilities presented below:

Programming capabilities on the second level "2. Experienced", all domains were required.

Tools capabilities on the first level "1. Beginner", only API were required from that domain.

Cloud capabilities on the first level "1. Beginner", only cloud storage was that domain.

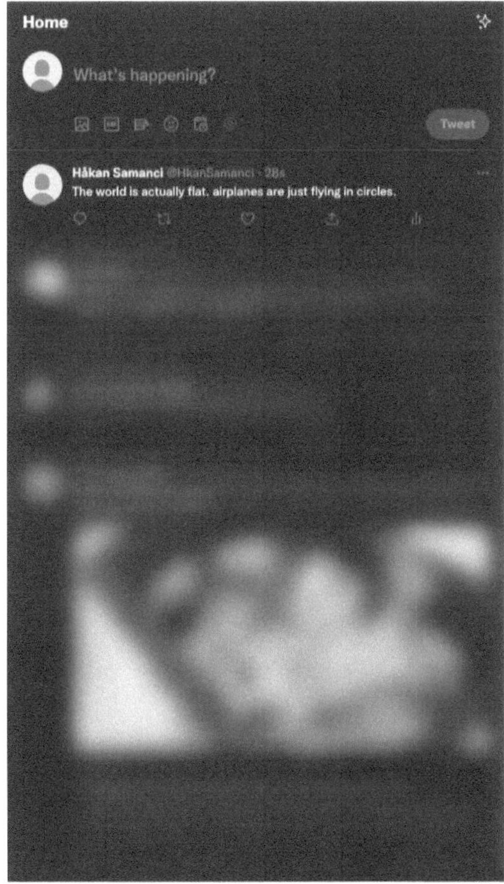

Figure 15: Twitter feed

5.3   Summary

The implementation of the bot was successful, a tweet was generated with a text input which was generated by a custom prompt via an API. All capabilities that were needed were on the lower end of the competence spectra, at "1. Beginner" or "2. Experienced" never reaching "3. Adaptive". General and Programming capabilities were required in their entirety. From *Cloud* both Hosting and Storage were needed and regarding *Tools* only API was required, all the other domains from these two capability categories were unnecessary. There was no need for *Math* or *Data transportation* capabilities since the bot that was implemented was more of basic character.

6 Analysis

This chapter analyzes the result obtained, section 6.1 analyses the formatted list of capabilities, section 6.2 analyzes in a closer look if the bot can be considered social. Lastly section 6.3 analyzes the capabilities required in the process.

6.1 Resulted capabilities

The first section 5.1 of the result represents a list of capabilities the authors would argue we possess, as third year students at Royal Institute of Technology (KTH) which is one of Sweden's most prominent technology universities and according to THE (Times Higher Education) international highly reputable[hög21] [Lim21].

The list only contains what was gathered from looking at the courses we took during these three years, all except one domain. The domain *General* with its two-subdomain *common sense* and *problem solving* are subjective and relative. We did acknowledge the problematic nature of judging it but deemed it as a very necessary capability to take into consideration. This leads to a situation where the validity of this specific capability *General* could be disputed.

All capabilities gained outside of university were disregarded as well as the grade. Only the capabilities deemed necessary were included in that list. To paint a picture what were excluded *Multi variable calculus* and *Mechanics* were two of many courses. The claim is that the result is a nonbiased list of capabilities, we the authors holds, with a credible source backing our claims.

6.2 Our social bot

The resulting bot was functional in many domains. These functions relied on multiple API:s but OpenAIÃs API stood for the main part of the execution and simple logic made it qualify in our mind as *social*. The availability of these API created a scenario where a much more advanced social media bot could be created, all the functions were created and implemented with a simple while loop and multiple *if* statements. We only created the logic, the rest was handled by the APIs.

Financial burdens were obstacles for available functionalities, in theory the bot could run for an infinite amount of time. Either set time intervals or a trigger-based system requiring essentially no human interaction at all if necessary. The bots behavior could be influenced simply by adding key parameters like *Angry Happy*, *Concerned* or *Deceptive*. The possibility to feed data manually, like a list of words to generate randomized text for tweet's or taking another accounts tweets data to generate the response to a specific tweet. It had the ability to monitor users and hashtags, retweeting their content based on a specific topic, even the *mood* of the tweet can be analyzed and only retweeting a specific narrative.

As our intention was to implement a social bot, we had to ensure that it could act in different ways and fulfil some requirements. As stated in section 3.4.1 (where the criteria for a social bot are presented), this assurance is covered by the Moscow model.

Must have (what must be included): A social bot must have the ability to [GG18]:

Profile: Have a profile of some representation: Twitter account

Follow: Follow user accounts: Twitter API + Programming logic

Follow back: Able to follow and unfollow other users who start follow the bot: Twitter API + Programming logic

Retweet: Share other user's content: Twitter API + Programming logic

Add Tweet: Create basic own topics and share content: Twitter API + OpenAI API + Programming logic

Follow tweet: Follow content of specific topics: Twitter API + OpenAI API + Programming logic

Quote: Quote other users' statements: Twitter API + Programming logic

Use hashtags: Utilize hashtags to find desired topics: Twitter API + Programming logic

6.3   Required capabilities

Our social bot was successfully deployed on the internet, with a set of simple functionalities. This was accomplished through the executed steps illustrated in section 5.2. The required capabilities were less demanding than we had anticipated, mostly since Twitter and OpenAI had their APIs available for the public.

Several capabilities were required in the process and considering the evaluation criteria presented in section 3.4.2, these capabilities ranged from *Beginner* to *Experienced* in some cases. Why it did not extend beyond these areas was of the nature our social bot possessed. No general AI models were necessary or any advanced functions which would make the bot act more on its own. Instead, capabilities regarding, problem solving, analyzing, and programming was underlying the success.

In the end we successfully created a more complex social bot (functionality wise) than we anticipated possible with our set of capabilities. This can have some serious implication and arises the issue of whom can judge the requirements. What we indicate with this is that there potentially is a larger gap between the perceived requirements and the actual requirements needed regarding an implementation of a social bot.

7 Discussion

This section will further discuss gained experience and outcomes from the gained result. Section 7.1 discusses the potential harm our social bot could have performed followed by section 7.2 where a discussion regarding our thoughts on the level of required capabilities and dangers it may pose. Lastly, section 7.3 will discuss stated validity threats and how we managed to pass them.

7.1 Potential for harm

To our surprise, it existed in several contexts a potential for harm, much due to the fact that there is a wide market of available APIS on the internet today which decreases the level of competence and capabilities required which makes it more manageable to implement a social bot. For instance, Twitter offered an API portal, available for any user who requested for it. This made the process to get started manageable if you could read and follow the given documentation. The potential for harm could be made by analyzing private data from other users on twitter, this could be accomplished by utilizing a method called web scraping. Web scraping is a method for extracting data from website[20]such as Twitter. This method was available and could be added to our bot but required far more work. Since this was not stated as a requirement for our bot the be categorized as social and the Twitter API was available, no web scraping was performed.

Similarly, for OpenAI, their API provided us with functionality that could be expected from an PHD student if that's even enough since OpenAI has a whole team of researchers and are heavily funded, backed by investor such as Microsoft [dea15]. Even though the full inventory of OpenAI models is not available to the public, the parts that are, are well advanced [Ope22a]. If these parts would be added to the bots infrastructure, potential harm can be made but it is up to the creator if it will do so. Oftentimes these models are misused, utilized to create political stigma and polarization [Ass+20]. Where the ability to label something positive or negative opens many potential outcomes. With just some simple if statement logic the creator has the power to spread information that only fits their agenda and suppress any opinion not sharing the same view.

7.2 Required capabilities

As stated previously our perception of what would be required by us was an overestimation to say the least. That estimation came from someone with three years of higher education in the field of computer science. The reason for this assumption was because we misjudged the wide range of available resources on the internet, from Twitter API portal to OpenAI. These instruments were of fundamental help and made the implementation easy to manage.

What is problematic is that a social bot can be used as a tool for spreading malicious intent which already has been established in US election 2016, US election 2020, Annexation of Crimea to name a few [Bla22] [SEN17] [Nad20]. The truth is simply this, sadly social bots has been weaponized and the question that remains is who have access to these weapons.

First our result proves that the absolute *highest* bar is set at, is considerably lower than three years of studies that the university provided us with. We would estimate that a reasonably motivated individual with *problem solving* and *common sense*, but no programming experience could potentially deploy their own social media bot.

Second, looking at the results and our miscalculation, we could not accurately estimate what was required. How are people with no technical background supposed to do it. This might become an issue with legislative organs not fully understanding the seriousness of the situation. What we end up with is a judicial system that do not have the capacity to stop what is happening right before our eyes. No laws that can be enforced means that people who are able to find a way to exploit the situation can wreak havoc and there is nothing that can be done about it.

7.3   Validity threats

There were four different validity threats stated in section 3.5, acting as guidelines for truthfulness and validity for this study. These four threats were: (1) *Credibility*, (2) *Transferability*, (3) *Dependability* and (4) *Conformability*. Below a detailed description of how these threats were handled are presented.

Credibility: Is a measure of trustworthiness [Håk13], that the gained result is to be viewed reliable by others. This was ensured by during all phases of the exploratory pre-study every literature reviewed and utilized was supported by academia and published within scientific journals. Furthermore, as we the authors were subjects, a well-documented implementation process was presented with set criteria, this to ensure a transparent contribution of what literally was required by us to implement the resulting bot.

Transferability: Is a measure of generalizability of the resulted findings [Håk13]. The idea is that a transferable piece of information should be usable in another article or concept regardless of in which context it was originally used. Usually, a limitation of qualitative studies is that they lack generalizability. However, to ensure that this was not regarded as a limitation, all the work through the method as well as the implementation phases was documented as thoughtful as possible. For this study to be able to be transferable a transparent process had to be performed. With this in mind, the documentation includes all resources, instruments, sources, tools and capabilities that was required and utilized.

Dependability: Is a measure of reliability [Håk13]. Regardless of how many times the same study is performed, the results should remain the same. The dependability of judging the correctness from the conclusion of this study can be hard, since our study is of an explorative and qualitative nature, it is hard to replicate the results. Though if the study is performed through the same environment, utilizing the same tools, an implementation of a social bot can be succeeded and correlations in the conclusions as well.

Conformability: Is a measure of objectivity [Håk13]. In other words, it is a confirmation of the results by others. In our case we the authors were the research subjects which indicates that all selected capabilities as well as used tools was chosen by us. To confirm the validity of these assumptions several criteria for what a capability is and what a social bot should be able to accomplish was stated and followed. Unfortunately, no third-party subject has analyzed and confirmed the function of the resulted social bot instead the process is documented step by step in this book.

8 Conclusions

In this work we investigated which capabilities as well as tools that were required to implement a social bot on Twitter. This was done by *exploring* available literature and resources to take *actions* to implement the social bot. Since the implementation was successful and listed requirements was fulfilled, the bot was considered social as well and was able to interact with other users on Twitter.

In the first chapter of this work, we state the approached problem, purpose, and goal. The goal could be seen as two sub-goals where the first part was conveyed as:" The *goal of this book is to map what capabilities are required to implement a social bot, in order to understand who is able to implement one.".*

This part of the goal was clearly met since the overall picture of what is required in the process to implement social bot is well documented and presented in the work. But it has the potential to be more specific and narrower in future works. To understand who can implement a social bot from available resources form the internet there has to be other subjects with different background of experience. However, the experience from this work indicates that the capabilities required to implement a social bot are well within reach of a third-year Bachelor student in the field of computer science. Which in a way can be seen as societal progress since if one who is educated has good intentions they can contribute with their knowledge and use a technical instrument such as a social bot for sustainable purposes. But on the other hand, if their intentions are bad, one can infiltrate and do potential harm to the societal conversation by manipulating public opinion and polarize the conversation on social media platforms.

The second part of the goal was conveyed as:" We *wish to help further studies regarding bot detection methods by delivering a base of capabilities."*

This part of the goal was partly met, since we concluded how manageable it was to gain advanced functionality, thus potentially requiring the detection scope to be wider than expected. However, an attempt to present the appropriate capabilities suitable for the implementation is presented but for it to be considered a base is misleading. Further studies have to be made and compared to get a bigger picture of the capabilities required. The conclusion to be drawn is the fact that all resources used in this work was available free on the internet. This could indicate that the capabilities and competencies required for one to implement a social bot is more manageable than one can expect.

8.1 Future work

This study only focuses one type of subjects (we the authors) which possesses experience and competence within the field of computer science and based on our experience and capabilities, it was surprisingly manageable to implement the resulting social bot and all the features that came to follow. On the other hand, it is difficult to draw any proper conclusion regarding people with less experience in a technical field such as computer science, therefore it would be appropriate to expand this study where you instead test subjects within a lower competence or skill level. Through this, one could draw further conclusions regarding who can implement a bot, how they navigate themselves and which instruments they choose to use. This would have been of interest as several of the resources available have a hidden, underlying agenda. If the person performing such an implementation is not aware of it, devastating consequences can occur. Why this is of interest is mainly based on what is conveyed in the introductory chapter *Target group*, as bots have become a significant problem for many actors, new policies would be relevant. These policies should questionize the current *degree of difficulty* or *competence threshold* for those who should be able to access and implement an advanced technical instrument that a social bot is.